What Is Ravi Good At?

by George Ivanoff

illustrated by Richard Watson

OXFORD
UNIVERSITY PRESS
AUSTRALIA & NEW ZEALAND

Everyone in Ravi's family
is good at something.

What is Ravi good at?
What does he like to do best?

Ravi's sister loves playing football.
She is really fast and strong.

Ravi is not.

Ravi's mum is a teacher.
She is good at maths and spelling.

Ravi is not.

Ravi's dad loves to bake cakes.
He is really good at cooking
and baking.

Ravi is not.

Ravi's little brother has
a guinea pig.
He is really good at looking
after it.

Ravi doesn't like guinea pigs.

What is Ravi good at?

What does he like doing best?

Ravi loves listening to music.

Ravi is really good at singing.

Ravi is joining the school choir!